How to Make Money Investing in Pre-IPO Stocks

An Investor's Guide to Building Wealth in Private Companies

Manny Fernandez
& Josh Maher

This book is presented solely for educational and entertainment purposes. The author and publisher are not offering it as legal, accounting, or other professional services advice. While best efforts have been used in preparing this book, the author and publisher make no representations or warranties of any kind and assume no liabilities of any kind with respect to the accuracy or completeness of the contents and specifically disclaim any implied warranties of merchantability or fitness of use for a particular purpose. Neither the author nor the publisher shall be held liable or responsible to any person or entity with respect to any loss or incidental or consequential damages caused, or alleged to have been caused, directly or indirectly, by the information or programs contained herein. No warranty may be created or extended by sales representatives or written sales materials. Every company is different and the advice and strategies contained herein may not be suitable for your situation. You should seek the services of a competent professional before beginning any improvement program. The story and its characters and entities are fictional. Any likeness to actual persons, either living or dead, is strictly coincidental.

TABLE of CONTENTS

PROLOGUE

Authors Manny Fernandez and Josh Maher met while Josh was researching the best investors in the world for his book *Startup Wealth: How the Best Angel Investors Make Money in Startups*. Josh wanted to interview Manny after he was named SF Angel Investor of the Year in 2014, and he was instantly impressed with both the entrepreneurial and investment success Manny had achieved. That interview led the two to become friends and to Josh becoming an investor in Manny's company DreamFunded.

Since then, Manny has been named 1 of 33 entrepreneurs to watch in 2016 by Inc. Magazine and has received the Equity Crowdfunding Leadership award. Using DreamFunded, founders, employees, and other stockholders have sold shares of companies such as Dropbox, TaskRabbit, LiquidSpace, Lyft, Revel Systems, and more. Josh published that book, and it continues to receive rave reviews from entrepreneurs and investors seeking to understand just who *seed stage investors* are.

In this book for new and aspiring individual investors, Josh and Manny explore the legal, theoretical, and practical aspects of investing in pre-IPO stocks. The research and writing of the book was a joint effort between the two authors, and their findings are narrated from Manny's perspective.

Manny is a sought-after keynote speaker on equity crowdfunding and the pre-IPO market. His appearances range from sharing the stage with super angel investor Dave McClure at the East Meets West conference in Honolulu in 2016 to appearing on CNBC's Squawk Box to inspiring a Shark Tank-style television show in

Canada to borrow the name of his company, DreamFunded. You can find him on social media @MannyFernandez.

Josh is an international keynote speaker and lecturer on early stage investing and raising capital. His talks and research reflect his passion for improving transparency in the fundraising process. You can find him on social media @JoshMaher.

1

DISCOVERING the PRE-IPO MARKET

A s a young entrepreneur, I dreamed of building a business like Bill Gates or Steve Jobs had. I dreamed of building a big business and having the status and power that came along with that level of success. Starting in real estate at the right time, I did build a successful business, and I created enough wealth to finance startups and entrepreneurial firms. However, I attribute my present success to a serendipitous event that helped me understand what was missing from my earlier vision and what changes were necessary in the market microstructure to enable employees and other stakeholders of entrepreneurial firms to realize their dreams before their firms transitioned from startup to growth companies. More on the missing parts of my vision later. Permit me to reminisce briefly for a moment...

During my days in real estate, I found that I had a knack for connecting with people, and I built a wide network of colleagues who were chasing similar dreams. At the time, my network of friends and colleagues were all chasing dreams of building the next Facebook or the next Apple. Many within my circle of friends eventually became a who's who of entrepreneurs in Silicon Valley.

Leaving my successful career in real estate, I began financing some of the best companies my friends were building, as well as my own, and my network of savvy technologists grew rapidly. The companies at this stage are generally referred to as *startups*: from zero to eight or nine years old, these are companies that are attempting to create new value in the world. After such a company is certain that it can create greater value and profit from the marginal value it creates year in and year out, it becomes a growth company. It is the promise of greater values from current values that propels a startup into becoming a growth company. Most of the young employees at these firms are bright, well-educated, and motivated people. They go to work for persuasive technologists and business leaders with a dream. They work for a lower salary, hoping that they'll be a part of building that dream company into the next global leader, and, at the same time, building their own wealth. Most of these startups didn't eventually succeed. But more than a handful of them did.

The journey was similar for those who did not make it and for those who did: fourteen-hour work days, seven days a week, with little time for the other pleasures life has to offer. When growth is the most important metric used to convince new investors that the investment will pay off, then all of life's luxuries need to be placed on hold in the early days of a company's life. This is fine for the young technologists whose efforts do result in building an incredible company. When the companies they work for transition from the startup stage to a growth company, they usually have a capital infusion from a significant private investor, an acquiring company, or the sought after initial public offering (IPO). When the capital infusion occurs, those entrepreneurs along with their employees can cash out, and the payout gives them the flexibility to build a lifestyle that they never would have been able to enjoy when they started working at the startup all those years ago.

Success so defined is not the norm for all startups. It has been reported that over the course of the first ten years of a company's origin, 71% of all startups fail (Statistic Brain, 2016). The employees who worked for those unsuccessful companies went through the same journey as the employees who happened to be at the successful ones. The difference is in the final payout: zero or millions.

People like to share their stories, whether we're at the gym, in coffee houses, in pubs, or at restaurants. We like to tell the tale of our journey to colleagues young and old. My circle of friends was mostly the younger, hungrier techies who were learning from the older ones. They'd always heard more stories about failure than success. The dream was still alive, and they wanted better outcomes. Why would they want to work night and day, for half a decade at a growing company, only to find that the company wouldn't make it? Only to find that they'd built their life around the success of a failed company? Stuck in the middle of a pond with no paddles to get ashore?

Not all companies fail: many continue to grow. But growth does not always translate to personal wealth for employees working in growing firms. Even employees of unicorn companies can find themselves in different boats floating in the same pond. *Unicorn companies* is a term coined by venture capitalist Aileen Lee in a well-regarded TechCrunch article researching companies that were private and valued at over a billion dollars (Lee, 2013). Finding a way to exit the early startup stage and enter the growth stage becomes more difficult despite the fact that valuations on a growing number of companies are in the billions. Unicorn employees find themselves wishing their lives weren't on hold and often are frustrated at only dreaming of having access to all the wealth they see on paper. Even a portion would do wonders for their lifestyles: allow them to send their kids to a private school or to buy a house to raise a family in.

The great entrepreneurs that many look up to—the Bill Gateses, Larry Ellisons, and Jeff Bezoses of the world—all built wildly successful companies and quickly IPO'd before growing to the massive size that they are today. They provided liquidity to their early employees in a way that the private unicorns of today aren't doing. As I noted, today there are companies with billion dollar valuations that are still private and have not provided their stakeholders the opportunity to monetize their gains.

Bill Gates led the formation of Microsoft in 1975, and by March of 1986, he took the company public providing liquidity to investors and employees alike (Microsoft, 2016). Eleven years to go public seems like a long time in comparison to the eight years it took Mark Zuckerberg to take Facebook public (Facebook, 2016). By comparison, companies such as Palantir and SpaceX are going on thirteen and fourteen years with valuations in the billions already.

Microsoft, Oracle, and Amazon never reached valuations like Facebook, Palantir, or SpaceX did in the private markets. Facebook's IPO was a record-setting valuation for an initial public offering: shifting the bulk of the value creation that employees are responsible for to the earlier, less liquid, time period of the company's life.

There is also the issue of mobility. When employees are working for lower salaries and want to change jobs, they're usually forced to choose to buy their options or forfeit them. Many forgo the option purchase, because they simply can't afford the options even after working five to seven years for a company. So they leave the company without the benefit of the stock that represents the value they created. If the company had gone public, or if there was a secondary market for the stocks on which they could sell their shares before the company went public, then the employee could afford the option purchases out of the proceeds of the secondary market transaction. This is why employee access to those shares is so critical.

By 2012, my network was increasing quickly. It included an array of entrepreneurs who were building incredible companies and a strong collection of investors interested in alternative asset classes. This is when the serendipitous event that I referred to earlier happened.

It was one of the members of the angel group that I founded, SF Angels Group, who approached me and asked if I wanted to invest with him in Twitter. I wasn't aware of any financing round that Twitter was undertaking and was surprised that there would be an opportunity to invest.

The investor told me that employees, founders, and early investors had been selling their equity in startups and entrepreneurial firms for years to private investors to get liquidity ahead of any type of exit that the company went through. This market—the buying and selling of companies' stock before they went through their transitions from startups to growth companies—had been hidden from my view, and I was intrigued. That such a possibility existed in the market place had not crossed my mind.

That weekend, I took a break from tech and investing to spend time with family and friends. We were watching boxing on television, and everyone pulled out their phones to participate in the Twitter feed. That's when it clicked for me. Twitter had truly penetrated every corner of society: from young to old, from early adopter to mature market, and from non-tech savvy to tech savvy. It dawned on me that the market potential for such transactions was huge.

I started talking to other investors: some of whom had never invested in this pre-IPO market that I was discovering and others who had. Everyone who had never made a pre-IPO investment told me to stay away from it because they believed that the brokers would be the only ones who made any money. The investors who had invested in the past wanted to know how they could get in on the deal.

I researched the company and the market. I realized that Twitter had gone from a handful of early adopters to a mainstream customer base and that this might be the best opportunity available to me to profit from their success. So I invested.

But I didn't invest enough. My investment turned out to be wildly profitable. Just a few short years later, Twitter's IPO returned multiple times my investment to me.

When Twitter exited, I realized that I'd built an amazing network of friends and colleagues who were accumulating massive wealth on paper, and they were all starting to sell those shares to institutional investors and to a growing number of angel investors. Access to these companies and employees was one thing: having a large enough check to make it worth their while was another.

It is access like this that enabled Chris Sacca to reach billionaire status. Now a well-known TV personality on the television show Shark Tank, Mr. Sacca decides the fate of upcoming entrepreneurs on a panel of the richest men and women in the world. And it all started with access. His access, like mine, was access to the best entrepreneurs in the country and to the employees whose wealth is locked up in the stock of the unicorn startup companies they work for.

It is access to these startup companies, and investing in secondary offerings of the companies' stock before the companies transitioned through IPO or acquisition into a growth company, that brought incredible wealth to Chris Sacca. It is this pre-IPO market for stocks of startup companies that we want to share with you in this book. It is a fascinating investment opportunity for small and large investors alike. But market participants are only beginning to know about the promise of this new market for equity investments. Read this book, and you'll know more than most participants in this relatively new market.

2

WHAT IS the PRE-IPO MARKET?

After one successful exit, I wanted more. I started researching potential companies and began talking to institutional and angel investors and to entrepreneurs and employees at tech startups. After many conversations, I began to better understand the typical participants in the pre-IPO market. It's filled with lawyers, institutional investors, founders, and employees trying to capture some of the value that they create in the world before their respective firms go public.

This market starts with the founders. Startup founders incentivize new employees with stock options. This added incentive is usually in addition to salary that covers the employee's basic living needs but not much more than that. The employee is there to build the shared dream and welcomes the opportunity to participate in the upside when the company is eventually successful. Investors have seen how well this works and encourage stock options as an incentive. Stock options give the employee the right to purchase common shares of the company at a pre-specified price. The common shares are different from the preferred shares that investors in the company receive. The common shares are a single class of stock with no special preferences such as the right to be paid first when the company exits.

Early investors receive special preferences as a way to compensate them for taking early risks. As the company continues to grow, there is less risk in making an investment in the company. The reduced risk attracts different types of investors who have different levels of risk they're willing to tolerate. Sometimes those investors invest in traditional financing rounds such as a Series D, Series E, Series F, or Series G round. The letter indicates the number of financing rounds that have occurred in the past. The word series indicates that newly issued preferred shares with a certain set of preferences were issued. Sometimes those investors invest in shares being sold by employees, founders, or investors.

For a variety of reasons, lawyers get involved when it comes to these secondary transactions. The company wants to restrict or control who owns shares of the company. The common shares may have a right of first refusal clause. The investor may want to establish value and need the company to participate in due diligence.

In September of 2011, Twitter engineered a transaction that involved many of these attributes. Twitter was founded in 2006, and by 2011, many early employees were sitting on great sums of wealth. On paper. The company was huge, valued at $3.7 billion in December of 2010, and was getting ready to raise financing to get to an IPO in 2013. Five years of hard work from founding to this moment in 2011, and the employees had made a tangible impact on the world. Twitter was one of the tools used earlier that year during the Arab Spring pro-democracy movement that unfolded in Egypt as the world watched on. Employees would be asked to push harder for two more years, until the IPO, and many more after that to satisfy impatient public market investors. Employees at Twitter were facing life decisions like the rest of us make—around families, homes, education, aging parents, and so on—and wanted a way to access even some of their share of the $3.7 billion valuation.

Working closely with investors, Twitter engineered a Series G financing round under which half of the round—$400 million—was invested into newly issued preferred shares from the company (the Series G preferred shares) and half of the financing round was used to purchase existing shares from employees and existing shareholders. The investors who made the $800 million investment included T. Rowe Price, J.P. Morgan, Chris Sacca, and others. In addition to buying shares from employees, several early investors sold some of their shares in the transaction. The financing round more than doubled the value of the company at the same time—at $8 billion—making the share price for employees around $16.

Twitter allowed employees to sell up to 20 percent of their shares in the offering: and some did, some didn't. Receiving $16 a share for stock that they initially received for pennies is a great payout for employees. As for the investors who purchased the shares for $16? By June of 2014, the stock hit a high of $69, which left plenty of room for investors to receive a profit. At the IPO, those same investors would have paid almost double at $26 a share. On the first day of trading, they would have paid $44 (Tsotsis, 2011).

Investing just $5,000 in September of 2011 and then selling a year after the IPO in November of 2014 for $41 means that your $5,000 would turn into more than $12,000, more than doubling your money in just three years.

Practically, could you have invested just $5,000 into the secondary offering of Twitter's shares? No. If you weren't an institution like T. Rowe Price, or didn't have access like Chris Sacca, you would not have the opportunity. And even if you did have access, you'd also have needed to allocate many multiples of that $5,000.

Company-organized transactions are still rare. Most companies don't want to spend the energy and the hassle of putting together an offering in the way that Twitter did. Pulling together the transaction itself is costly, it takes time, and the benefits are hard to measure. Companies like NASDAQ and Dreamfunded.com are working to address these company-organized transactions. Other companies are also trying to address this opportunity through complex derivative transactions that attempt to address employee-initiated transactions. These are great solutions for institutional investors and hedge fund members who don't have the same clout or connections as T. Rowe Price or J.P. Morgan.

The rest of the investing population simply doesn't have the capital, access, or legal horsepower to understand these complex transactions. Investing $5,000 into Dropbox, for example, isn't something an investor can just go do on these platforms. Minimum check sizes are multiples of that, and the fee structures make the cost of these transactions even higher.

Not all is lost, though. As I said in the first chapter of this book, the wealth creation power of investing in secondary shares is something I want to share with you. The federal government does too. On December 4, 2015, President Obama passed the Fixing America's Surface Transportation Act (the FAST Act). Yes, it is a bill about roads; however, a provision in the bill, Section 4(a)(7), tagged on at the end to get the provision into law before the end of the year, added a new exemption to securities law. This new exemption makes it easier for founders, employees, consultants, and investors to sell the shares of a private company they own. The law gives stockholders an *exemption* from registering the stock with the Securities and Exchange Commission (SEC) in order to sell the stock.

There are a variety of exemptions and rules around who needs to register a stock for sale before actually selling it. For example, the exemption that allows you to sell publicly traded stock to another investor without first registering that stock yourself is provided by Section 4(a)(1). Other exemptions are outlined in Rule 144 and Rule 144A.

Meeting the requirements of the new Section 4(a)(7) exemption are much easier and enable a greater degree of flexibility on the part of the stockholder and for the markets where transactions like these take place. To meet the requirements of the new exemption, you simply have to have a reasonable belief that the buyer is an accredited investor, be selling shares that are included in a class of shares that have been authorized and outstanding for more than 90 days, not publicly soliciting buyers, not be considered a bad actor by the SEC, and be able to provide the buyer, at his or her request, basic relevant information from the company that issued the shares. Basic relevant information includes things such as the last two years of financial statements and details about who controls the company.

Under the old rules, an employee who chose to exercise the stock options would have to first exercise the options, paying cash to the company for the shares at whatever price the options gave them a right to purchase them at. Then they'd have to wait 12 months, so their wait to purchase a home for their family, for example, could feel like an eternity. Next, if they could sell the shares 12 months later, they'd have to pay any applicable taxes on the gain.

The question of whether or not they were allowed to sell previously had a vague answer. The old exemptions made it more difficult for buyers and sellers to connect due to ambiguity around general solicitation, definitions of brokers in the exemptions, and the notification and timing requirements. The old exemptions were not broadly used, which leaves wealth tied up in private companies for an extended period of time.

The government recognized that there was a problem, and organizations like NASDAQ began to lobby the government to loosen regulations to make it possible for a real secondary market to emerge. This stock market—where all of the company shares being traded are privately held companies—is a market that has been hidden from view for most investors for far too long. With the passage of the bill, employees now only have to wait 90 days to sell their shares. This shortened time period reduces the tax burden and begins to put the power back into employees' hands.

In the last few years, this wasn't the only regulatory change to open up investing in startup and pre-IPO companies. Employees also needed to be empowered to sell their shares, and you, the investor, needed to be able to invest. A law called the Jumpstart Our Business Startups Act (the JOBS Act) was signed into law by President Obama on April 4, 2012. This law has a number of provisions to make it easier for companies to raise capital, make it easier for investors to invest in privately held companies, and make it easier for a pre-IPO market to emerge.

So, how has the passage of the JOBS Act affected the startups and the pre-IPO market? First and foremost, the act enables companies to stay private longer. For investors at the earliest stages of a company's life, this means the timeline for receiving a return will be much longer than in the past. The way the JOBS Act does this is by increasing the number of shareholders a company is allowed to have. This increase—from 500 to 2000 shareholders—makes it easier for companies to issue stock to employees and investors.

Prior to 2012, when companies began to grow, the number of employee shareholders and investor shareholders couldn't exceed 500 without triggering strict disclosure procedures that effectively forced the company to operate like a publicly traded entity. The government recognized this as a limiting factor to growth and allowed companies to quadruple the number of shareholders. This increase in the number of shareholders also alleviates the pressure placed on management when employees want to sell their shares on the pre-IPO market. Even if every employee at a 450-person company sold some of his or her shares to one other person, the company can still double in size before bumping up against the 2000-shareholder limit.

Second, the act addresses the question of access to capital: making it possible, after a more than 80-year hiatus, for non-accredited investors to invest in privately held companies. Title III of the JOBS Act is commonly referred to as Crowdfunding (not to be confused with crowd-sourced capital or pre-sales that are transacted on platforms such as Kickstarter). This crowdfunding allows anyone to invest in private companies. When this access was closed by the Securities Act of 1933, it was specifically closed because so many people at the time were being swindled by dishonest people fraudulently selling shares of privately held companies with little to no financial disclosure or insight into company operations. The unsuspecting public invested and lost large sums of money. To stop the madness of the crowds back then, the Securities Act forced companies to either register the shares they were going to sell to the public with the SEC or meet one of the requirements that would provide the issuing company with an exemption.

Today, the JOBS Act has improved the exemptions available in a way that supports investing in both startups and pre-IPO companies. The main exemption that companies use for these unregistered, private offerings is Regulation D. Regulation D, or Reg D as it's commonly called, offers three sets of requirements that a company can meet to receive an exemption: the rules for those requirements are Rules 504, 505, and 506. The other, less commonly used exemption is Regulation A, also known as Reg A. Both sets of exemption rules received a significant refresh as a result of the JOBS Act, which mandated that the SEC make sweeping changes to improve the capital markets for innovative companies that fuel our national economy.

Reg A took on the most drastic changes in a new regulation nicknamed Reg A+ and focuses on companies that aren't the sort of high-growth companies that become pre-IPO, so we don't go into it here.

Reg D was also changed, and the changes are designed for the sort of high-growth companies that become IPO candidates. This part of the regulation opens the doors for you, the investor, to be able to invest a responsible portion of your portfolio into pre-IPO companies.

Rule 504 allows companies to sell up to $1 million of restricted securities within a 12-month period to any number and type of investor. Under Rule 505, companies are allowed to sell up to $5 million of securities within a 12-month period to any number of accredited investors and no more than 35 non-accredited investors. When non-accredited investors are in the mix, the company has certain reporting requirements that begin to look more like a public company. Although not as strict as the fully audited financial reports that a Tier 2 Regulation A offering requires, the potential amount of capital raised is also tenfold less than the Reg A offering.

To get anywhere near the $50 million allowed in Reg A, or the hundreds of millions of dollars required to truly finance the greatest companies that will reach pre-IPO status, companies must raise capital for their business based on the third and final rule: Rule 506. Rule 506 allows companies to sell an unlimited amount of securities to an unlimited number of accredited investors and up to 35 unaccredited investors. Although the unaccredited investors create the need for the same financial reporting as rule 505 creates, because of the amount of money companies may be raising, Rule 506 also requires an unaccredited investor be financially sophisticated.

With a term like *accredited investor*, you might think that there would be a big process, a test, or maybe even a ceremony for individuals to become accredited. In reality, to be accredited, a person must have earned $200,000 in the last two years (or $300,000 with a spouse) or have a net worth of over $1 million, excluding their personal residence.

The companies that enter the pre-IPO market have all raised capital under the Rule 506 provisions: raising hundreds of millions of dollars starting with a million or so at the earliest, riskiest stages and reaching investments in the hundreds of millions of dollars as they prepare for an IPO. Similarly, the markets such as NASDAQ and DreamFunded raise capital to invest in pre-IPO opportunities from investors based on this same Rule 506 exemption.

The JOBS Act forced the SEC to clarify how companies could or couldn't advertise when raising money. The worry was that dishonest people making fraudulent claims would have advertisements in newspapers for the next great investment opportunity in an attempt to swindle unsophisticated investors. For that reason, the SEC defined Rule 506(c) offerings as those under which the company raising money can publicly advertise; however, the company selling shares can only accept investments from investors who the company has verified as accredited investors.

Conversely, Rule 506(b) doesn't allow for companies to generally advertise the securities that they're selling. It also doesn't require companies to verify that each investor is an accredited investor. This saves the investor the trouble of having their certified public accountant (CPA) or financial advisor sign an affidavit regarding their status or providing two years of tax returns directly to the company. To see an example of companies raising capital under the 506(c) rules, go to the AngelList website without logging in or verifying your accredited investor status, and see what startup companies you can invest in. All of them are using a 506(c) exemption. To see companies raising capital under the 506(b) rules, go the DreamFunded.com website, log in or register as an accredited investor, and see what pre-IPO companies you can invest in. All of them are using a 506(b) exemption.

With the support of U.S. federal and state governments, startup and pre-IPO investing is becoming more accessible for both individuals and institutions. Collectively, more participation in the startup investment market and the pre-IPO investment market will increase innovation and job growth in the economy. High-growth companies drive employment, and innovative entrepreneurs can't build high-growth companies without capital. Institutional capital is entering the startup investment market at all stages, and online platforms are showing up to make this easier for them. Similarly, DreamFunded is providing access to pre-IPO and early startup investments for individuals who want to take advantage of this growing opportunity.

3

SPEAKING the LANGUAGE of the PRE-IPO MARKET

Now that you have a rough idea of what a pre-IPO market is, I'll review some of the key technical and definitional terms pertaining to the pre-IPO market and provide a brief history of the market. If you come across a term that isn't covered in this chapter, there are additional definitions provided in the glossary.

The term *angel investor* is an important one. The practice of angel investing didn't come from Silicon Valley or anywhere on the West Coast of the United States. It came, in fact, from a much larger hub of finance and innovation: New York City.

The term angel investing comes from Broadway, the principal theater district of the United States if not the entire world. The theater industry is filled with creative artists trying to connect with audiences. Sometimes shows are visionary and last for decades, and sometimes shows ride a short wave of momentum and capture the fad of the day. Creators need financing for their projects. Wealthy individuals, searching for brilliant talent and an engaging story that they would be proud to have their name associated with, pursue talent with a critical mind. The practice of wealthy patrons supporting creative artists started even before Broadway, but it was only on Broadway where wealthy individuals became colloquially known as angel investors and the name stuck.

The practice of angel investing dates back to the earliest of times, when companies operated mainly on trust, without any regulatory oversight. The original corporations that were formed during the pre-industrial era sent boats to foreign lands to bring back exotic goods, which were put together by people operating the vessels and investors looking for a return on their investments. There was no public stock market and no regulators: just some people who wanted to sail their ships to faraway places and bring back goods to sell at high margin returns and other people who wanted to partake in those returns. Back then, the risks were just as high as they are today: the ships could wreck, there were pirates, the captain of the ship could be dishonest, and the list goes on. We praise those early business-centered organizations as the first corporation-like entities that ever existed, and today we have formalized what a corporation is as a result of those initial angel investors and entrepreneurs (Ferguson, 2009).

Fast forward to the early years of the U.S. economy. Alexander Graham Bell took angel investments for his first company in 1887: well before the SEC formalized rules around a stock market and private placements. Investing in startup companies began to get more formal attention from the wealthiest of families in the United States, most of which operated out of New York City. Jack Whitney was the first to formalize his angel investing activity into a venture fund and created what we know today as venture capital (a subset of private equity).

We've since married the term angel investing with the practice of investing in startup companies. The term as it is used in North America doesn't span the Atlantic. In Africa, Australia, and Europe people say "business angel investing" to differentiate it from "theatre angel investing." In Asia, and South America, however, the term angel investing is used.

Angel investing is not inherently philanthropic: it is fundamentally capitalistic. The reason people get into angel investing may be because they are passionate about a particular idea; however, there is an expectation of a return on the investment for angel investors regardless of whether they are investing in the next great Broadway show, a restaurant, sustainable farming, or wireless power transmission (Gupta, 2000; Rose, 2014; Maher, 2015, June).

The SEC makes it easier for some investors to be angel investors and make it harder for others. The SEC makes it easy for people who meet the SEC's accredited investor requirements and harder for people who don't. To be an accredited investor a person must earn $200,000 annually ($300,000 combined with a spouse) or have a net worth of $1 million dollars (excluding the value of the primary residence). There are other provisions for professional investors, but this wealth measurement is the only measurement used by independent angel investors today.

The definition of accredited investor, and therefore who can easily become an angel investor, is rapidly changing. There are already provisions to allow non-accredited investors to invest. Further, the proof that someone is accredited is rarely verified by the SEC. There are also new rules being proposed in Congress in 2016 based on findings by the SEC on the accredited investor definition. These proposed rules would link the wealth measurement outlined above to inflation. They would also allow independent investors and professionals to test in to becoming accredited investors.

Regardless of the qualification that an investor brings to the table—accredited by wealth, accredited by test, or not accredited at all—the process of purchasing of stock from a company is essentially the same. The company issues stock, gives it to founders or employees as compensation, or sells it to investors. These are known as *primary transactions*. If any of those investors sell the stock to another party, the transaction is known as a *secondary transaction*.

The place where the primary transactions are tracked is known as a *capitalization table*, commonly referred to as the *cap table*. All of the shares issued, owned, and outstanding are tracked there. All of the shares that people have purchased or been granted are listed in the cap table, alongside all of the shares that have been set aside to grant later. Usually there are a few different classes of shares listed in this order: first, there are common and preferred shares, followed by multiple types of preferred shares that are tied to the round of financing. Next to the shares that have been purchased are the dollar amounts paid. Next to the shares that have been granted are vesting schedules with how much has been vested and how much still remains to be vested.

The purpose of the cap table is to show who owns the business and how much money has been invested. If convertible debt exists, it doesn't complicate the cap table, but debt is still a part of the capital structure of the business. At a future financing round, that debt will convert into equity and that isn't well represented on the default view of cap tables.

Another key concept that relates directly to pooling your capital with other investors and investing the sum is a concept called *carry*, which is short for *carried interest*. A carry is a share of the profits after the investors have had their initial capital investment returned. Unless you are familiar with the financial industry, neither term is intuitive. It would be much better stated as management profits, or share of profits, considering that these two sentences mean the same thing: "Each of the general partners at the venture capital firm receives a portion of the management profits." and "Each of the general partners at the venture capital firm receives a carry."

This book discusses pooling capital to invest in companies. Firms that facilitate the pooling of capital and ongoing management of the group of investors, such as DreamFunded, will take a carry in exchange for those services. The process of pooling capital through an online platform is known as *equity crowdfunding*, and it is a small sliver of the activity happening under the larger term crowdfunding.

Crowdfunding is a method of raising capital with the collective effort of many people for a specific project. Crowdfunding platforms raise money in the form of donations for all types of different things: from new products and services to social causes and public initiatives. Donations are often made in return for some sort of reward, such as a product, a service, or tickets to an event.

The term crowdfunding can be confusing, because it is used to describe both what is happening on websites like Kickstarter.com and to describe what is happening on websites such as DreamFunded.com. These websites leverage the capital of the crowd to fund an activity. However, pre-sales campaigns like those on Kickstarter are different than the equity investments that take place on DreamFunded. Kickstarter is an example of crowdfunding in which a crowd is pre-purchasing a product and then waiting a long time and hoping that the company can actually develop and build the product. If the company does build it, the product becomes available; however, funders don't participate in future growth. DreamFunded is a crowdfunding example of a crowd that is investing for equity and not purchasing any product. They are waiting a long time, and perhaps making introductions, giving advice, and so on, in the hopes that the company will grow and that they can participate in the growth of that company.

Investors who participate in equity crowdfunding to purchase shares from founders and employees in secondary market transactions are typically purchasing shares that were originally issued as an incentive to early employees. Like salary, stock is used to incentivize early founders and employees. Many of these shares are issued to employees through an employee stock option plan.

Many companies use employee stock options plans to compensate, retain, and attract employees. These plans are contracts between a company and its employees that give employees the right to buy a specific number of the company's shares at a fixed price within a certain period of time. The fixed price is often called the *grant* or *exercise price*. Employees who are granted stock options hope to profit by exercising their options to buy shares at the exercise price when the shares are trading at a price that is often much higher than the exercise price.

Companies sometimes revalue the price at which the options can be exercised. This may happen, for example, when a company's stock price has fallen below the original exercise price. Companies revalue the exercise price as a way to retain their employees.

If a dispute arises about whether an employee is entitled to a stock option, the SEC will ordinarily not intervene. State law, not federal law, covers such disputes.

These shares are initially issued to founders or employees and then vest over time. They can only exercise or sell shares which have fully vested. *Vesting* is the process by which an employee accrues ownership of stock in a company. The standard vesting terms in Silicon Valley are a four-year vesting cycle with a one-year cliff. A four-year vesting cycle means that the employee will be accruing stock in the company until the end of the fourth year: at which time all their stock options have been earned. A one-year cliff means that the employee will not begin accruing stock until the end of the first year. This prevents employees from leaving the company with stock options within the first year. At the end of the vesting period, the employee has the right to purchase all the vested stock from the company at a discount. Most tech companies in Silicon Valley are choosing to offer their employees more equity in lieu of a higher salary. More than 15 percent of the ownership of Silicon Valley's private tech companies is in the hands of the employees. The ability of early investors and employees to sell their shares in the companies that have awarded them the shares before the company goes public or transitions to another phase is the origin of the pre-IPO market that is becoming more common.

When investors purchase the stock of startups and pre-IPO companies, they build a portfolio or collection of investments that is sometimes referred to as an *early stage portfolio.*

At the core of a strong early stage portfolio, investors have only allocated 10% of their net worth to early stage investing. This protects the potential losses from losses drastically affecting their net worth. With that protection in place, there must be enough small bets into companies that have an option to have incredibly outsized returns. Most investors have come to the conclusion that 10 to 50 investments are required to make this work for early stage startups. With no *power law effect* where one or two investments return the entire early stage portfolio, pre-IPO-only portfolios can get away with far fewer investments and still achieve outsized returns.

Let's look at the average accredited investor who has a net worth of $2.5 million. If they allocate 10 percent to early stage investments, then they only have $250K total to invest. In a world where returns only happen in 5- to 10-year timeframes (or more), this necessitates careful planning and a lot of waiting to invest that capital over the course of several years. If you take that $250K and invest $5K (with another $5K for follow-on) or $10K (with a plan not to follow-on) into each startup, then you will have a portfolio of 25 companies. If these 25 companies are all invested in during the same year, you'll have to wait for a long time to see your investment returned and you will have ramped up your searching and evaluating skills for an activity that you only really do for a single year. Alternatively, if you invest in five startups per year, you'll have five years before you run out of your allocation and may, in fact, see returns that you can re-invest by the time you become fully invested.

If you really would rather invest all at once, the amount of time and effort to build the skill of finding great startups may not be worth it. It may make more sense for you to invest through an online forum like DreamFunded.com.

The *valuation* of individual companies determines the overall value of an investors' portfolio. A valuation is an estimate of a company's worth at any given stage of funding. It is the price at which the company should be able to be sold on the market. From a startup perspective, it determines the amount of money the founder will receive from an investor and what equity percentage he or she must give up in return.

4

INVESTING in the PRE-IPO MARKET

When investing in startup companies, many investors start by thinking about becoming an angel investor. They join angel groups, read books like *Startup Wealth: How the Best Angel Investors Make Money in Startups* (Maher, 2015), and start attending demo days from the local accelerators. Often investors are too busy to commit the time needed to both find great companies to invest in and support the companies they invest in. For investors with a responsible portfolio of 20 to 30 investments, the time commitment is 20 to 60 hours a week on their own (Wiltbank, 2012).

For some investors, the fun is in the mentoring, so they become mentors at accelerators such as Techstars, 500 Startups, and Y Combinator: investing in their funds and engaging as a mentor to the companies that the accelerators have chosen to help. For other investors, it's more about the returns and less about the mentoring. These investors come to platforms like AngelList to get exposure to the asset class of startup companies.

Whether you are investing with friends, joining angel groups or accelerators, or using crowdfunding equity platforms like DreamFunded.com, you are focusing on a small piece of the startup investment opportunity. These certainly offer the highest possible outcomes; however, they also have the highest possible failure rate and the longest time to liquidity. Investors in the earliest stages are forced there because the check sizes at the later, less risky stages are so large that most investors simply can't afford to participate. This leaves a difficult gap in the investor's portfolio: a startup investor often has to wait five to seven years before knowing if any of the companies she or he invested in even have a chance at exiting or becoming a pre-IPO company. As we saw in the case of Twitter, the first investors to invest in the company made an incredible amount of money. We also saw that the last investors in, even those who invested in the secondary shares of the company, also made a sizable profit. The only differences were how much of a return on investment they received and how long it took.

Because so many startups fail, nearly every experienced investor will advise that building a responsible portfolio means investing in 20 to 30 companies (Statistic Brain, 2016). Building a responsible portfolio of only pre-IPO companies or a combination of startups and pre-IPO companies doesn't need to be nearly as complex, because the risk of failure in the case of pre-IPOs is drastically reduced. Although some companies do file for an IPO and later cancel based on demand in the public markets for their shares, only a small percentage go on to closing their doors. Most find private market investors to finance growth, find an acquirer, or move to profitability and pursue a slower growth strategy. The risk of complete failure in the pre-IPO space low.

The failure rate at this stage is minor, and the return rate much smaller. Our independent research into 49 different portfolios with outcomes ranging from zero to three times the invested capital, the average return is still in the 28 percent range over 2–4 years. The 49 portfolios examined included sizes ranging from five to thirty companies with an average of eleven winners and five losers across all portfolios.

That's not a bad average; however, diversifying into a large pool of investments doesn't appear to add significant improvements to the return profile. This means that a portfolio of 5–10 companies should be able to get you similar returns compared to a portfolio of 20–30 companies. The reason for this is the structure in which you're investing. When you invest in a pre-IPO company, you're investing at the end of a long series of investments that have been made into the company. You're investing at a valuation that's been set by one of those previous investors. The only option for the company to return all of that capital and profits to the investors is to undertake a liquidity event in which you will be able to participate.

What happens if a pre-IPO company that you invest in, such as Dropbox or Airbnb, doesn't end up going public as planned? They continue to operate, likely raising another round of funds at potentially a higher valuation. Depending on the platform that you've chosen in which to make your pre-IPO investments, you may have the opportunity to re-sell those shares on a pre-IPO market. If you hold on to the shares, those new investors will still need to get a return from their investment, which means an eventual liquidity event for the company and you.

Let's look at what a venture portfolio that includes both startup and pre-IPO investments might look like. A venture portfolio that includes both startups and pre-IPO companies will eventually become a portfolio of only pre-IPO companies as the startups grow. If you invested in five startups five years ago, you'll still have to wait five to ten years for those companies to reach a point that they can exit the startup stage and transition into a growth company through an IPO, acquisition, or other means, but some of them will get there.

What happens in the interim? Later stage investors continue to invest in the company, diluting shareholders, and adding liquidations preferences. All of this creates an environment in which your compensation for early risk is only worthwhile if the company has a really great outcome. If the outcome is just mediocre, you may wind up with nothing in return.

In the following table, you can see where the transition from startup to growth-stage company occurs and how pre-IPO investing fits neatly at the end of that cycle with reduced risk as compared to seed and series preferred investments that traditional angel investors make.

Table 1: Access to short-term pre-IPO investments

- - - - - - - - - - - - - - - - - Company Size - - - - - - - - - - - >				
Company Stage	Startup		Growth	Mature
	Seed and series preferred	*Pre-IPO*		
Private or Public?	Private	*Private*	Private or public	Private or public
Duration	0–2 years 2–12 years	*2–4 years*	1–10 years	10+ years
Typical Investor	Friends, family, angels, venture capitalists	*Institutio nal funds, angels, and YOU*	Private equity, institutiona l funds, individual investors	Private equity, institutional funds, individual investors
- - - - - - - - - - - - - - - - - - Time - - - - - - - - - - - - - >				

A portfolio that includes both startup and pre-IPO investments would still need a range of 15–25 startups and 5–10 pre-IPO companies as the ratio of risk-to-reward of investing in those early startups isn't going to be improved by investing in pre-IPO companies.

Taxes are another matter. Investing in startups that meet the Qualified Small Business stock standard, as set forth in section 1202, can mean that the profits on the investment are tax free. This is a permanent tax break, thanks to the PATH Act of 2015. Although this is fantastic for investing in startups and can mean millions in additional returns, most pre-IPO company investments won't qualify for this tax break, because the aggregate gross assets of the company at the time of the investment are more than $50 million.

Your pre-IPO investment will be an investment that is taxed like most other long-term investments.

What are reasonable fees for these types of investments?

Fees to invest in the pre-IPO market vary depending on the vehicle that you use to invest. Usually you won't make a pre-IPO investment and be sent the actual stock certificates, even though the person selling the stock is handing over stock certificates. This is due to the liquidity in the market. Laws such as the FAST Act are new and market participants are still emerging and testing different models to find what works best.

Most models involve a special purpose limited liability company (LLC) being formed and the LLC is the entity that purchases the private stock. The LLC is purchasing the stock at the managing members' direction, who is taking direction from the members of the LLC. Investors who want to allocate capital to pre-IPO companies invest in these special purpose LLCs, and a manager is hired to handle the details through the life of the investment. Some of these LLCs invest in the purchase of stock from a single company to give investors the opportunity to pick the companies that they want to invest in. Other LLCs pool a number of investments together to give the investor an index of pre-IPO companies.

The hard cost to maintain the LLCs is minimal, costs include:
- Formation of the LLC with the state and federal governments.
- Annual licensing fees and tax reporting
- Validation of investor accreditation
- Legal fees related to purchasing and selling the stock

There is also the soft cost of human oversight:
- Gathering the group of investors
- Ensuring the investors have all information they need to make an independent decision
- Working with stockholders and company representatives on the sale of the stock
- The ongoing coordination of the investment

These are all real costs that need to be covered. Some are there only to support the pooled investment vehicle, and others are going to exist regardless of the pooled nature of the investment vehicle.

The fees to cover these costs are expressed in a number of ways. You'll see fees called sales fees, broker fees, success fees, administration fees, management fees, and carried interest. The amount of these fees will vary depending on the size of the investment capital being raised and the amount of liquidity in the market. Fees in this market have already come down dramatically from where they were even five years ago, fueling the move from an institutional-investor-only market to one where individual investors can participate in an online marketplace, such as DreamFunded.com.

Table 2: Typical pre-IPO market fees

Type of Fee	Purpose	Frequency	Percent
Administrative fee*	Covers all the hard costs listed previously	Annual	1–5%
Management fee	Operations	Annual	.5–2.0%
Sales fee (also called Broker fee or Success fee)**	Making the investment happen	One-time	2–7%
Carried interest	Managers' portion of profits	One-time	10–15%

* Some markets cover this out of management and sales fees.
** Not all markets have this fee.

If you find an opportunity where the LLC is charging all of these fees at the same time, you should walk out the door and not invest with them.

A reasonable fee includes just one of the annual fees and one of the one-time fees.

What should I do with diligence?

When looking at pre-IPO opportunities to invest in, there are several advantages that you have over investing as an angel investor in the first few rounds of financing. As discussed earlier, the risk reduction is one obvious advantage. When it comes to performing due diligence, there are a lot more advantages. The companies have been in business longer, they have lots of customers, they have lots of employees, and they've built a culture and reputation that will follow them through their IPO.

Most high tech pre-IPO companies have been in business for seven to twelve years and have grown the number of customers faster than most of their competitors. If they weren't able to grow faster and sustain that level of growth, they wouldn't be on the verge of taking a large capital infusion to allow them to truly enter the growth stage, and they wouldn't be a pre-IPO company.

Many sales will occur on the basis of Section(a)(7), brought to us by the FAST Act. This act allows the buyer to request up to two years of prior balance sheet and profit and loss statements. Being able to review two years of financial history and operations can give you insights into how the team manages the company and evolves their strategy.

Although not every investor prefers to spend hours poring over the company's balance sheets, the fact that the company has been around for so long also allows investors the ability to perform deeper research by looking at other public registrations. For example, you can look at SEC registrations, issued and pending patents, and corporate or domestic litigation. The ability to look at a multi-year history of even a young company allows the investor from her home—whether across the globe or next door—to perform diligence like she would for any other new IPO or mature company traded on a public exchange.

Investors can also read independent reviews of products online and can talk to customers in their network of colleagues, friends, and family. In many cases, you can talk to reviewers, or at the very least read reviews, from current and former employees on Glassdoor.com. Investors can research news, conferences, and other public media sources to get a sense of the culture within the company. Is it a culture that can continue to grow and scale? If the company were a year or two old, this level of diligence would be impossible and a deeper connection with the founding team would be required to make critical investing decisions that require this level of knowledge.

What should investors expect in terms of communication from management and annual reports?

Actually executing an investment in pre-IPO companies is slightly more difficult than buying stock on E*TRADE. It's pretty easy.

The pre-IPO transactions of yesteryear were offline, handshake- and martini-driven transactions. Today, most pre-IPO transactions happen through online markets. There are only a handful of online markets leading the pre-IPO market, and they are divided into those serving the individual private investors, and those serving institutional investors. All of today's online markets use some form of pooled investment medium, as described previously, and all share the same attributes when it comes to making an investment. With some major exceptions. The institutional markets are designed for institutional money managers. Because this isn't a book for institutional investors, the process as it pertains to those markets isn't covered.

For individual private investors, the process is simple. Investors register for an account on the market website; provide details about who they are, what they want to invest in, and what their accreditation status is; and finally meet with a representative of the market. Some markets will require tax returns or other information to be submitted. From there, investors browse investments and elect to be included when the investment deal closes. On closing, the investors electronically sign documents and wire or Automated Clearing House (ACH) transfer the funds. The final steps are filing the Schedule K-1 form with your taxes for a year or so and then depositing the returns after you sell the stock.

5

MANAGING a PRE-IPO PORTFOLIO

The wealth that can only be built by rapidly compounding high rates of return is one that is available in the pre-IPO stock market. In the past, investors in this market were already well-connected and wealthy individuals. Thanks to the work to make these investments more accessible to more people, less well-connected investors are already gaining access to these opportunities. Investors of all ages can benefit from investing in this asset class. Turnaround times of just a few years and 200 to 300 percent returns are unheard of in the public market. Even investing in the IPOs themselves is riskier than pre-IPOs. In the case of Twitter, both an IPO investment at $23 a share and investing in the public market when the shares began trading at $44 were under water in January of 2016 with the shares just above $16.

Well-educated professionals with an interest in gaining better access to the wealth created by the IPO process are flocking to the asset class. Many are working professionals with full-time jobs, families, and an interest in high tech companies. Others are investing in startups but still lack access to the opportunity to invest in pre-IPO companies. With over 114 private tech unicorns waiting for the right opportunity to IPO today, there are thousands of employees desperately wanting to cash out a portion of their equity to afford the million-dollar price tags on most homes in Silicon Valley (CB Insights, 2015). CB Insights, in their 2015 Tech IPO Pipeline report, estimate that there are 588 venture-backed companies that will likely be thinking hard about going public within the next few years depending on business and market conditions.

CB Insights had identified 590 tech companies in their 2014 Tech IPO Pipeline report. Of the companies on the list, 43 percent of them had exited or raised additional capital within a year. Sixty-seven companies or 11 percent exited by IPO or merger for an aggregate value of over $33 billion. And 192 companies had raised financing totaling over $12 billion.

Across 2015, investing in the S&P 500 would have created practically no additional wealth. The market opened and closed around the same place despite a year of ups and downs. If just a small percentage of your portfolio was exposed to the pre-IPO market, the 11 percent that exited within the year would have given your portfolio an edge in the market that isn't directly correlated to the movement of the market overall.

IPOs do require a market willing to finance the offering; however, those financiers are generally the growth funds, such as those at T. Rowe Price and J.P. Morgan (as discussed earlier) participating in the pre-IPO market. Those funds are designed to invest in quality companies, with significant growth, and a clear path to profitability. Market corrections may slow the path to IPO, but the underlying company growth is what dictates the value and appetite for investors with cash on the sidelines.

It doesn't matter whether your net worth is parked in an index fund, a robo-advisor, or some other more elaborate scheme. The data referenced in Chapter 4 regarding the 49 portfolios examined suggests that adding pre-IPO investments to your portfolio is the safest mechanism for investing in privately held companies.

Let's examine three portfolios to see how a pre-IPO allocation can improve your returns. We'll examine pace, how often investments should be made; size, what percentage to allocate; diversity, both of private stock and the rest of the assets in the portfolio; and account types.

Example 1: an index-oriented portfolio

The first portfolio we'll look at is the simplest. A basic allocation between stock and bond indexes with an eye for low fees. This first portfolio will be the smallest: a portfolio of $2 million.

Prior to adding any privately held companies to the portfolio, let's run down how the capital is allocated. A traditional 60 percent stock and 40 percent bond strategy has returned an average 15-year annualized return of 9.4 percent (the median was 9.6%) with a high of 13.2 percent and a low of 7.3 percent, according to research done by Ben Carlson and Ritholtz Wealth Management (Carlson, 2014). Table 3 represents a simplified view of this type of allocation.

Table 3: Modern 60/40 portfolio

Asset	Allocation
U.S. stock market fund or exchange-traded fund (ETF)	36%
International stock market fund or ETF	24%
U.S. bond fund or ETF	28%
International bond fund or ETF	12%

To add pre-IPO investments to a portfolio like this, reduce U.S. stock exposure by 5 percent, international stock exposure by 1 percent, and U.S. bond exposure by 4 percent. With a portion of any total U.S. stock fund or ETF, your portfolio is already exposed to IPOs and other growth companies that attract a similar type of investor as pre-IPO investments do. These investors often invest in both equity and debt instruments of companies at this stage. To accommodate adding pre-IPO investments directly to your portfolio, reducing some of your exposure to these markets is the logical place to look. Your new allocation is outlined in Table 4.

Table 4: Modern 60/40 portfolio with an allocation to pre-IPO stock

Asset	Allocation
U.S. stock market fund or ETF	31%
International stock market fund or ETF	23%
U.S. bond fund or ETF	24%
International bond fund or ETF	12%
Pre-IPO stock	10%

Just a small shift in your portfolio could increase your total return by almost 2 percent. With the decision to allocate 10 percent of your total investment portfolio to pre-IPO stock, the next logical question is "How do I go about allocating that capital?" In our example $2 million portfolio, you have up to $200,000 to invest in pre-IPO shares and will need to wait 2 to 4 years to get any one investment returned to you. It's important to decide how often you want to make investments. Allocating $50,000 per year, for example, would allow you to invest in 1 to 10 companies every year, depending on how active you wanted to be finding and making investments.

To simplify, if you're making five investments a year in pre-IPO companies, then you're spending one to two months leisurely researching an opportunity, talking to friends about their use of the product, and deciding to make an investment. That's a fairly comfortable pace, and it allows you to sell existing holdings at the right time as well as spread the new investments over a longer part of the business cycle.

The other component of diversity is the industry factors. If you're already using index funds or ETFs to diversify your portfolio across industries and geographies, then including a wide array of industries and sectors in your pre-IPO portfolio would be prudent. This can be difficult to do. The current pooled investment vehicles that invest in a number of pre-IPO companies allow you to make a single investment decision; however, they may not provide industry diversification simply due to the type of companies they have access to. You may wind up with a pre-IPO fund investment that includes all enterprise information technology (IT) software companies, for example. Carefully selecting the companies in your pre-IPO portfolio allows you to ensure that you've diversified the types of companies that you're invested in.

Investing in pre-IPO companies directly from a savings account or tax advantaged retirement account is possible to do; however, companies at this stage are too large to qualify for the 100 percent tax exclusion for sales of qualified small business stock held for more than five years (up to $10 million). Without special treatment, investments from a traditional savings account would be considered long-term capital gains and thus taxed at 15–20 percent, depending on your income level plus an additional 3.8 percent Net Investment Income Tax.

If you invest using a traditional individual retirement account (IRA), the investments are made with capital that you've never paid taxes on and the returns grow tax free, allowing you to compound them at a higher rate. You aren't required to pay tax every time you sell the shares that you invested in after the company exited. Instead, all of the profits are available for you to re-invest until the point in time that you begin taking distributions from the IRA. Those distributions are taxed as income instead of as long-term capital gains.

Investing through a Roth IRA means investing with capital that you've already paid taxes on at your current income rate. As long as the investments have been held for more than five years and the withdrawals are being taken after you've reached age 59½, the gains both compound tax free and are tax free upon withdrawal.

Here's a quick recap assuming that you re-allocated $200,000 across four years and re-invested the profits, 200 percent every four years, across sixteen years.

Savings. After every exit, you'd pay at least 23.8 percent on the profits, totaling nearly half a million dollars. Your $200,000 would grow to just over $2 million.

Traditional IRA. After every exit, you'd just keep investing. If you were in the top tax bracket while taking the profits out after sixteen years, you'd end up with $1.9 million. On the other hand, if you were earning less income in your later years, and fell into a lower tax rate, then your profits would be closer to $2.3 million.

Roth IRA. After every exit, you'd keep investing, as in the case of the traditional IRA. Assuming that you met the criteria outlined previously when you took the withdrawals, you'd still pay no additional taxes and walk away with closer to $3.2 million.

If you take into account the initial taxes paid on the capital in the cases of the savings account and Roth IRA and the returns for the different account types, then savings, traditional IRA, and Roth IRA would change from $2 million, $2.3 million, and $3.2 million to $1.2 million, $2.3 million, and $1.9 million, respectively.

Example 2: a stock-picking portfolio

The second portfolio we'll look at focuses on finding the next major trend in the economy and profiting greatly from it. If you're investing in high-growth public companies, such as Uber, then this portfolio may look familiar to you. This second portfolio is slightly larger than the first: a portfolio of $5 million.

Before adding any pre-IPO investments, let's first look at the allocation. Table 5 represents an allocation for an example investor who likes to pick hot companies to invest in and has been well rewarded for doing so. This person may work with professional traders to get ideas for his collection of 15–25 stocks and usually hold these stocks for months to years depending on the trend. Adding to this growth or momentum seeking, investors in this category are more interested in other alternative investments, such as hedge funds or venture capital (VC) funds. Depending on the skill of the investor in selecting companies or investment managers, a reasonable return is around 11 percent.

Table 5: Example stock picker's portfolio

Asset	Allocation
Collection of 15–25 stocks and options	38%
U.S. stock fund or ETF	16%
Long-term stock 1–5 yr	18%

holding	
Hedge fund or venture fund	28%

To adjust this portfolio to allow for 10 percent pre-IPO investments might make sense; however, considering the historical returns in each asset category is prudent. If you or the fund manager you selected are achieving top percentile of returns, then you probably shouldn't reduce as much of your allocation in that category. It's unlikely that both you and the managers that you're investing with are achieving top percentile returns at the same time, so a critical look at which category you're farthest from earning an average of approximately 15 percent annually in is a place where you should consider adjusting a little.

In addition to the return requirement, look at the companies being invested in. If you've invested in a venture fund that invests in late stage companies, adding more pre-IPO companies to your portfolio may not make sense. Liquidating your venture fund investment instead of allocating more capital to a late stage venture fund, you could replace that allocation directly with pre-IPO companies and likely pay much less in fees.

Similarly, if your collection of stocks includes many early initial public offerings, you should consider how different those investments are from a pre-IPO investment. As outlined earlier, an investment in Twitter at the pre-IPO stage would have been much more profitable than investing in the IPO itself or post-IPO on the public market. Consider shifting that allocation of early momentum growth stocks to just a little earlier in those companies' lifecycles, and you'll have a considerable impact on returns. Table 6 shows what a model adjustment may look like.

Table 6: Example stock picker's portfolio with an allocation to pre-IPO stock

Asset	Allocation
Collection of 15–25 stocks ad options	31%
U.S. stock fund or ETF	16%
Long-term stock 1–5	18%
Hedge fund or venture fund	25%
Pre-IPO	10%

The shift in allocation would improve returns. However, not as drastically: 1.7 percent in this case. The previous guidance on diversity and which accounts you should be investing in still applies. There is one thing to add. Unlike the previous index-oriented portfolio, a stock-picking portfolio investor, like this one, will likely feel more at home picking the handful of great companies instead of building a larger index of pre-IPO investments.

Example 3: a value-creating portfolio

The third portfolio we'll look at represents a carefully crafted mix of value-creating holdings. If you're investing in Berkshire Hathaway stock, this portfolio may look familiar to you. This third and final portfolio will be the largest: a portfolio of $10 million.

Table 7 represents an allocation for an example value-creating portfolio. This portfolio also gets the addition of real estate with an average return of 11 percent as represented by the return from 1992 to 2012 of the NAREIT Index. This average return of real estate investments improves the value-investor's portfolio returns slightly to 12 percent on average. Beyond this change, the portfolio doesn't look too drastically different from the second portfolio. If you're not investing in real estate today and want an online investing solution, try RealCircle.com.

Table 7: Example value-investor's portfolio

Asset	Allocation
Collection of 15–25 stocks and options	38%
U.S. stock fund or ETF	16%
Real estate	30%
Hedge fund or venture fund	16%

Similar to the second portfolio, this portfolio could benefit from the same critique of past returns to search for a place to find capital to re-allocate. The other thing we'll introduce into the re-designed portfolio is an allocation greater than 10 percent. Although investing in the first few financing rounds of a company comes with such great risks that an allocation greater than 10 percent presents too much risk for 90 percent of investors, investing at the pre-IPO stage decreases much of that risk. Table 8 shows what an adjustment may look like.

Table 8: Example value investor's portfolio with an allocation to pre-IPO stock

Assets	Allocation
Collection of 15–25 stocks and options	31%
U.S. stock fund or ETF	16%
Real estate	28%
Iledge fund or venture fund	0%
Pre-IPO	25%

While this is a drastic shift—removing all of their managed fund investments in preference for a pre-IPO allocation—this would make a lot of sense if the funds they are investing in are investing mostly in pre-IPO companies already and charging higher fees for the same investments. Going to a 25 percent allocation to pre-IPO investments does generate a much larger impact on the total return, boosting it by nearly 5 percent on average.

The advice related to diversity and account types from the second example portfolio applies to this portfolio as well.

The one commonality across of all these portfolio adjustments is that the allocation to pre-IPO companies is not entirely correlated to the public market. This lack of correlation can both improve your portfolio return and help you sleep better at night.

6

EXITING PRE-IPO INVESTMENTS

The final stage of a pre-IPO investment is the exit. Exits happen in a few different ways. In the worst case scenario, the company could fail and close its doors. Under more favorable circumstances, the company could get purchased or make an acquisition of its own.

Although there are many paths to exiting a pre-IPO investment, predicting the path that a company will take a few years before the exit can be difficult. At DreamFunded, we take a unique approach to analyzing the opportunities and attributes of firms that get listed in the market. We're only looking for high tech startups as a mechanism to filter for rapid growth and fewer dishonest people seeking to perpetrate fraud.

Pre-IPO investments can be great for your overall portfolio: they aren't magical enough to never fail, however. While failure is rare, some companies that are great pre-IPO candidates never make it. Looking critically into the number of companies preparing for IPO that eventually never make it, the number of tech companies in this category is very small.

Getting purchased is usually what happens to pre-IPO companies that never make it to the actual IPO. The actual process for a company to be purchased can take a very long of time. The actual purchase price depends on a long list of factors, including customer or market expansion, comparable pricing, technology innovation, human capital, revenue growth, and competitive bids.

You can see how deciphering the valuation of an acquisition in a short book like this one becomes difficult. What you do have available to you as a pre-IPO investor is comparable valuations. The simplest view is one that public market investors use; they take the acquisitions that have occurred in the industry or sector and divide that by the amount of annual revenue the company last reported. This gives investors a multiple of revenue to value the company with. If the company in question is well outside the norms of the revenue multiple that comparable firms in the industry were able to attain, the acquisition has a lower probability of getting done.

Reverse mergers and mergers of equals are much less common and much more difficult to predict or evaluate. Given a choice between the two, you'd certainly be rewarded for the merger of equals in more cases than a reverse merger. That said, both occur in tech startups much less frequently than a traditional acquisition or a traditional IPO, with reverse mergers being the less frequent of the two.

The IPO has been the mainstay for companies seeking maturity and the ability to have a long, enduring relationship with investors all over the world. Staying private certainly is possible; however, the lack of liquidity, the limit on the number of private stockholders, and the increased cost of capital push companies to consider a public offering. NASDAQ has a great tool (see http://www.nasdaq.com/markets/ipos/) for researching the companies that are filing to initiate a public offering. The tool allows you to get a sense of the fact that there really are only a few hundred high-tech, high-growth companies that go through an

IPO over the course of three to five years in the U.S. The relatively small pool of companies that achieve an IPO, or are considering it, have a few similarities:

1. A base of strong customer and revenue growth.
2. A firm understanding of the revenue, expenses, and timing of cash flows.
3. A sales, marketing, and distribution strategy that is reliable and replicable.
4. Significant headway in developing or penetrating a market.
5. An opportunity to win the market or become a leader in the market if the cost of capital is low enough.

Some companies that have all of these attributes find the combination of distribution and cost of capital from an acquirer is a much better deal for the company than going public. Other companies who have the best control of all five of these qualities choose to go public when the timing is right for them as a company.

From a practical perspective, the exit opportunity is straightforward. Companies that exit through an acquisition sell for cash, stock, or a combination of the two. If you invested in a pre-IPO company that goes this route, you may end up with a pile of stock from a publicly traded company. At that point you can choose to sell or hold onto your shares to get the returns into your bank account and begin re-investing in the next great pre-IPO opportunity. With either a stock offer or a cash offer, you'll receive paperwork to sign and a check. If your investment was made through a traditional savings account and not a Roth or traditional IRA, then you'll most likely note the profits to your tax advisor and report the earnings as long-term capital gains. If you're making these investments from an IRA, you'll just roll the profits back into your IRA and keep reinvesting. For more on using self-directed IRAs, see Self Directed IRA on Josh Maher's website (http://joshmaher.net/category/sdira/).

Failures and write-downs also have practical implications. If you get half of your money back and make no profits, the losses can be claimed on your taxes, assuming that you were investing in something other than a tax advantaged account such as an IRA. The best strategy for which account to invest from, and how to handle the taxes, is unique for most people, so use the contents of this book to have a longer conversation with your tax advisor.

7

WHY PRE-IPO? WHY NOW?

Most companies that went through a public offering between the years 1999 and 2001 were just zero to five years old, according to research published by Andreesen Horowitz, a prominent Silicon Valley venture capital firm, and Capital IQ, a market research firm. For companies that went through a public offering between 2012 and 2014, the average age of such firms clustered around five and ten years, with very few zero to two-year-old companies making an initial public offering (Andreessen Horowitz, 2015, June).

This research highlights one of the most critical shifts to our economy with regard to investing in innovative companies. The ability of investors to finance innovation and value creation has shifted from the public to the private markets. An investor in Microsoft could have achieved around 200 times their initial investment between the original financing of the company and the time the company went public. However, Microsoft then went on to create value upwards of 600 times more than that those early investors could have achieved, leaving an incredible amount of value for public market investors to capture.

Let's look at another tech titan with less history: Facebook. Early investors could have achieved closer to 800 times their initial investment while public market investors would need Facebook to be worth $45 trillion, nearly three times the U.S. gross domestic product (GDP) at the time of this writing, to achieve a return comparable to the one that Microsoft investors could have achieved.

It doesn't stop with these two giants. Apple, Oracle, Amazon: all have created massive amounts of value and wealth for investors as publicly traded companies. LinkedIn, Yelp, and Twitter, on the other hand, have struggled to offer these same outsized returns after going public.

The wealth, value, and jobs created in the economy has shifted in a major way to private companies. Venture capitalists, institutional investors such as insurance companies and pension funds, and the U.S. Congress have all recognized this shift. Regulation is slowly catching up with the shift, and it's these regulatory changes that are empowering you, the individual private investor, to participate in wealth creation in new ways.

According to a study by the Kauffman Foundation (Kauffman Foundation, n.d.), new businesses account for nearly all net new job creation and almost 20 percent of gross job creation, whereas small businesses do not have a significant impact on job growth when age is accounted for. Companies less than one year old have created an average of 1.5 million jobs per year over the past three decades.

Creating new jobs is only the start of the cycle. Those early employees need to be compensated for the risks that they're taking by joining a new firm that is creating things that have never existed in society before but may nevertheless fail. That compensation has historically come from liquidity events such as mergers and public stock offerings. But that might be too long for the economy to benefit the most and create the optimum number of jobs.

For job creation to affect the economy in the positive fashion that is taken for granted so often, value creation needs to be unlocked sooner for founders and early employees. This is where the importance of the pre-IPO market arises. It permits the early unlocking of value in firms that are constrained to stay private for a long time. If you want to participate in growing the economy with a portion of your investing portfolio instead of playing the zero sum game of the stock market, this is where you need to allocate some of your capital.

Institutions and large family offices have already shifted their allocations to include pre-IPO investments. Private investors finally have the opportunity now to begin making this same shift using platforms such as DreamFunded.

Between 2012 and 2015, Congress passed the JOBS Act, the FAST Act, and the PATH Act, all of which incorporated rules and regulations to improve the investment environment for startup companies. With this level of attention being paid by regulatory authorities to strengthening these private transactions as a permanent and growing part of the overall economy, the risk of investing in such markets is substantially reduced.

First it was the adoption of motorized vehicles, then televisions, and then smartphones. Now, investing in private markets is on the verge of becoming the norm. In a world where starting a company with an idea is relatively inexpensive, and access to a global customer base is quickly achievable, the phenomenon of enormous value creation in the economy has shifted to the private markets. Now that the financial system is incorporating this shift into the aggregate economy, more of us can finally participate in the system and generate wealth sooner rather than later.

RESOURCES for
FURTHER STUDY

There are a number of important resources mentioned and references made throughout the book. To make money investing in pre-IPO stocks, an interest in and proficiency for self-study is a must. To support your continued research and learning, here is a collection of recommended resources and a list of the studies mentioned in the book.

Recommended resources

First, there is http://DreamFunded.com. We recommend signing up, creating an account, and exploring the opportunities there.

Second, to show our appreciation to those who read *How to Make Money Investing in Pre-IPO Stocks*, here is an exclusive discount code to purchase a print version of *Startup Wealth* at 20% off the cover price. At https://www.createspace.com/5761590, use code NN28A6LT.

The following links are mentioned directly in the text of the book and are worth exploring in detail:

- The a16z presentation outlining the transition of wealth creation from public markets to private ones is at http://www.slideshare.net/a16z/state-of-49390473.
- Research about upcoming IPOs can be found at http://www.nasdaq.com/markets/ipos/.
- Learn to set up and manage your own self-directed IRA to invest in startups and pre-IPO companies at http://joshmaher.net/category/sdira/.

- Learn about venture debt at
  http://avc.com/2011/07/financings-options-venture-debt.
- To explore and learn more about online investing in real
  estate, visit RealCircle.com.
- To hear what real employees have to say about a company,
  visit Glassdoor.com.

Works cited

Andreessen Horowitz. (2015, June). "U.S. Technology
    Funding—What's Going On?" Retrieved from the *Slideshare*
    website at http://www.slideshare.net/a16z/state-of-
    49390473.
Carlson, B. (2014, February). "The Rick Ferri 60/40 Portfolio."
    Retrieved from the *A Wealth of Commonsense* website at
    http://awealthofcommonsense.com/2014/02/rick-ferri-
    6040-portfolio/.
CB Insights. (2015). "2015 Tech IPO Pipeline Report." Retrieved from
    the *CB Insights* website at https://www.cbinsights.com/tech-
    ipo-pipeline.
Facebook. (2016). "Company Info." Retrieved March 01, 2016, from
    the Facebook website at https://newsroom.fb.com/company-
    info/.
Ferguson, N. (2009). *The Ascent of Money: A Financial History of the
    World.* Penguin Books.
Gupta, U. (2000). *Done Deals: Venture Capitalists Tell Their Stories*.
    Boston: Harvard Business Review Press.
Wiens, Jason Jackson, Chris. (2015, September 13). "The Importance
    of Young Firms for Economic Growth." Retrieved from the
    Kauffman Foundation website at
    http://www.kauffman.org/what-we-
    do/resources/entrepreneurship-policy-digest/the-
    importance-of-young-firms-for-economic-growth.
Lee, A. (2013, November 2). "Welcome To The Unicorn Club:
    Learning From Billion-Dollar Startups." Retrieved from the
    Techcrunch website at
    http://techcrunch.com/2013/11/02/welcome-to-the-
    unicorn-club/.

Maher, J. (2015, June). "The Origins of Angel Investing." Retrieved
        from Josh Maher's website at
        http://joshmaher.net/2015/06/11/the-origins-of-angel-
        investing/.

Maher, J. (2015). *Startup Wealth: How the Best Angel Investors Make
        Money in Startups.* Seattle: Booktrope.

Microsoft. (2016). "Facts about Microsoft." Retrieved from
        Microsoft.com March 1, 2016 at
        http://news.microsoft.com/facts-about-
        microsoft/#ImportantDates.

Rose, D. S. (2014). *Angel Investing: The Gust Guide to Making Money
        and Having Fun Investing in Startups.* Hoboken: Wiley.

Statistic Brain. (2016, January 24). "Startup Business Failure Rate By
        Industry." Retrieved from the *Statistic Brain* website at
        http://www.statisticbrain.com/startup-failure-by-industry/.

Tsotsis, A. (2011, September 8). "Twitter Closing Its $400M
        Secondary Offering Tomorrow." Retrieved from the
        Techcrunch website at
        http://techcrunch.com/2011/09/08/twitter-closing-its-
        400m-secondary-offering-tomorrow/.

Wiltbank, R. (2012, May). "Returns to Angel Investors in Groups."
        Retrieved from Robert Wiltbank, PhD at
        http://www.willamette.edu/~wiltbank/seattle_angel_confere
        nce_may_2012.html.

GLOSSARY

accelerators

Programs for entrepreneurs that usually make a small capital investment along with a defined period of support and assistance for their business. Usually accelerators are three- to six-month programs and focus on driving customer-focused design and access to the top mentors and investors to develop a company that investors will invest in.

ACH transfer

When money is moved from one bank account to another bank account using the Automated Clearing House (ACH) network. Banks choose to participate in this electronic network to process check, debit, credit, and other batched transactions.

angel group

An organized collection of angel investors (such as Sand Hill Angels or SF Angels Group) that finds, researches, and invests in startup companies. Annual membership fees for a typical angel group are around $3,000 to $5,000. The average size check that an investor in an angel group writes is between $25,000 and $50,000 per investment.

asset class

A collection of investments that are similar. The similarity may be based on attributes of the investment, such as liquidity or risk, or based on the regulatory environment that governs the investment, such as accredited-investor requirements.

bad actor

An investor or investment advisor who the SEC determines is unfit to make or advise on investment decisions. The SEC makes the determination based on whether a person in a position to advise on investments has been part of a disqualifying event, such as certain criminal convictions, certain court injunctions and restraining orders, and suspension or expulsion from membership in a self-regulatory organization (SRO), such as FINRA, or from association with an SRO member.

capitalization

The capital structure of the business: where the money came from and what was exchanged for that money. A business may have a capitalization that includes common and preferred stock as well as bonds or other debt instruments.

common stock

A type of security that represents an ownership stake in a company. In certain circumstances, common stockholders have the ability vote on company policies and elect members for the board of directors. This is different than preferred stock, which private market investors generally invest in.

deal

Sometimes the term *deal* is used to refer to an investment.

due diligence

The Angel Capital Association (ACA) defines due diligence in the venture industry as the investigation and analysis that an investor performs to see if an investment opportunity meets the investor's criteria for funding. For angels, as well as venture capital firms, the primary objective of due diligence is to mitigate investment risk by gaining an understanding of a company and its market as well as determining the suitability of the investment for the portfolio.

employee stock option plan

According to the SEC, many companies use employee stock option plans to compensate, retain, and attract employees. These plans are contracts between a company and its employees that give employees the right to buy a specific number of the company's shares at a fixed price within a certain period of time. The fixed price is often called the grant or exercise price. Employees who are granted stock options hope to profit by exercising their options to buy shares at the exercise price when the shares are trading at a price that is higher than the exercise price.

Companies sometimes revalue the price at which the options can be exercised. This may happen, for example, when a company's stock price has fallen below the original exercise price. Companies revalue the exercise price as a way to retain their employees. If a dispute arises about whether an employee is entitled to a stock option, the SEC will not intervene. State law, not federal law, covers such disputes.

exit

The period of time in which a company is leaving the startup stage of its life and entering the growth stage. The exit from startup to growth can happen through IPO, acquisition, merger, or another private investor. See Table 1 in Chapter 4 for more details.

FAST Act

On December 4, 2015, President Barack Obama of the United States signed the Fixing America's Surface Transportation Act (aka, the FAST Act) into law. Primarily a bill about roads, and also referred to as the Highway Bill, it also contained a new exemption to securities law that was tagged on at the end of the bill to get the provision into law before the end of the year. This new exemption allows employees, consultants, and investors to easily sell the shares of a private company that they own. The law gives stockholders *an exemption* from registering the sale of stock with the SEC.

fund

A legal entity (usually an LLC flow-through entity) that manages money from investors looking for private equity in startup and later-stage companies with strong growth potential. Investors in the fund own units of the fund and the fund itself holds equity in the private company (the investment). The fund has a general partner (GP) who manages all operations of the fund and acts on behalf of the members of the fund, the limited partners (LP).

information rights

An investor's legal entitlement to financial and other information relating to a company that he or she is investing in, such as quarterly and annual income statements, balance sheets, and cash flow statements. Information could also include budgets and budget reconciliations, a dashboard of key metrics, as well as notices of material litigation.

JOBS Act

On April 5, 2012, the Jumpstart Our Business Startups Act (JOBS Act) was signed into law by President Barack Obama. The JOBS Act was signed with the intention of putting more capital in American startup companies to stimulate job growth. The most notable of these acts is Title III, also known as Crowdfunding. In May of 2016, Title III of the JOBS Act will allow over 240 million Americans (97% of the U.S population) to invest in private companies for the first time in more than 80 years.

limited liability company (LLC)

The easiest corporate formation to use when pooling funds to make an investment. It is also sometimes used by companies that take investments; however, that is less common for growth-oriented startups and more common for non-growth (flat cash-flow generating) startups. It is technically a company in which owners and managers enjoy limited personal liability and some tax benefits and avoid some restrictions associated with S corporations. The tax benefits are why it is bad for growth-oriented startups (an investor may report some pretty major losses on their taxes the first few years and then have to report their share of the huge upside) and good for flat cash-flow generating startups (pass-through losses and profits are a non-issue).

liquidation preference

How much of a return the preferred shareholder receives before common shareholders receive anything. The preference can be one times (1x) the original investment (the norm in 2016 so that the preferred shareholder at least gets his or her money back before any common shareholders get anything) all the way up to any number the VC wants (could be 2x, 3x, 10x, and so on).

If you are an early investor and are going to end up with a 2x liquidity preference and no participation preference, your $25,000 investment will only ever be worth $50,000, regardless of how great the company does. This may be great if the company was acquired or went public at a valuation that barely returned the $25,000 to $50,000 before the proceeds from the liquidity event were used up. This may not be great if all the common shareholders received 10x their investment because there was so much money left over after paying preferred shareholders.

NASDAQ

A company that manages several stock exchanges and is the first company to build a fully electronic exchange. The word NASDAQ came from the company's first exchange, created in 1971 by the National Association of Securities Dealers (NASD). They named that first exchange "National Association of Securities Dealers Automated Quotation". Today, NASDAQ continues to list over 3,400 companies and recently has been working on institutional investments in private companies. Beyond these functions, NASDAQ operates a number of markets throughout the world.

net worth

A simple measure of financial value that is calculated by adding up all of a person's assets and subtracting all of a person's debts. However, for the purposes of the SEC's definition of accredited investor, this calculation excludes the value of your private residence. So if you have $500,000 in cash and stocks, $1 million in equity in your home, and $50,000 of debt, then your net worth would be $1,450,000 yet you would not qualify as an accredited investor based on your net worth because the SEC would exclude the $1 million equity in your home. For more information, see *accredited investor*.

non-accredited investor

A U.S. investor who does not meet the SEC requirements for income or net worth to be classified by the SEC as an accredited investor. For more information, see *accredited investor*.

PATH Act

The Protecting Americans from Tax Hikes (PATH) Act was signed into law on Friday, December 18, 2015 by President Barack Obama. The law puts many tax breaks that were being extended every year into permanent law. Many tax breaks are specifically for small and growing companies. Others are specifically for investors in small and growing companies.

pre-IPO

A shorthand term that means "before the initial public offering," it refers to the time before a private firm becomes public. A pre-IPO *company* is a business, an ongoing concern, that is at the end of the startup stage and will soon be entering the growth stage. A pre-IPO *investment* is the purchase of stock in a pre-IPO company. A pre-IPO *market* is a place where buyers and sellers of pre-IPO stock meet to transact business.

preferred stock

A class of equity ownership in a company that has a preferential claim on assets and earnings over that of common stock. All preferred stock converts into common stock when a private company goes public during an IPO.

primary investment

An investment made directly into one of a company's funding rounds (for example, seed round, series A, series B, etc.). Primary investments are typically made through incubators, angel groups, VC firms, and equity crowdfunding platforms.

private placement memorandum (PPM)

A document that outlines the investment of a private stock offering. This term can also be used to describe any sort of private investment offering, but for the purposes of this book, it refers to offerings of private stock to accredited investors.

A PPM lays out for the prospective client almost all the details of an investment opportunity. The principal purpose of this document is to give the company the opportunity to present all potential risks to the investor. A private placement memorandum is, in fact, a plan for the company. It plainly identifies the nature and purpose of the company.

registration rights

This is simply the investor's legally viable ability to either force the company, after a period of time, to register the investor's shares and offer them publicly or to include them as part of a registration and public offering made by the company or a management stockholder. In other words, the investor can make the company include the investor's shares for sale on the public market just as they have done with their own common shares. Each class of issued preferred shares must have its own registration rights. This may mean that some shares never get registered by the company. If the company doesn't handle the registration, it is usually far too costly for the investors to register them by themselves.

restricted securities

Documents that represent the holder's ownership interest in a company where the ownership comes with certain limitations. They typically bear a restrictive legend clearly stating that an investor may not resell them in the public marketplace unless the sale is exempt from SEC registration requirements. Rule 144 under the Securities Act of 1933 provides the most commonly used exemption for holders to sell restricted securities. To take advantage of this rule, investors must meet several conditions, including a six-month or one-year holding period.

Even if an investor has met all the conditions of Rule 144, she still cannot sell her restricted securities to the public until she's had the legend removed from the certificate. Only a transfer agent can remove a restrictive legend. But the transfer agent won't remove the legend unless the issuer consents—usually in the form of an opinion letter from the issuer's counsel to the transfer agent.

If you want to remove the restrictive legend, you should contact the company that issued the securities—or the transfer agent for the company's securities—to ask about the procedures for removing a legend. If you have a broker, you may want to ask your broker to help you.

If a dispute arises about whether a restrictive legend can be removed the SEC will not normally intervene. The removal of a legend is a matter solely at the discretion of the issuer. State law, not federal law, covers disputes about the removal of legends.

right of first refusal clause

A provision that is often associated with the issuance of stock in a stock purchase agreement that allows the issuer the first opportunity to re-purchase the stock if the party that issued the stock to decides to sell the stock.

robo-advisor

A computer algorithm that takes the place of a human broker or human investment advisor.

secondary investment

An investment made into the stock of a company through a secondary source (not the company directly). If an investor purchases shares of a private company from an early investor or employee who owns the shares, then it is a secondary investment. Secondary investments are sold on secondary markets.

Securities and Exchange Commission (SEC)

The governing body responsible for creating and enforcing securities laws in the United States of America.

Securities Law of 1933

The Securities Law of 1933 was the U.S. government's answer to the stock market crash of 1929. The law changed the way that securities were sold and is the piece of legislation that created the SEC. Prior to this legislation, selling stock in a company was governed by individual states. This law moved the regulation under a federal umbrella that companies selling securities had to begin complying with in addition to their state regulations.

seed round

Typically, this is a startup company's first round of funding, and it comes before the company has a valuation. Typically, startups in Silicon Valley and elsewhere use a convertible note to raise money from investors during their seed round. The convertible note then converts to equity during a subsequent round of selling preferred stock.

Series A, Series B, Series C

The name for each new issue of stock that a company sells during its lifetime. Series A, Series B, Series C, and so on, is the way that financing has been organized since the early days of investing in new companies. Each series represents a new financing with formal filings with the SEC and is generally based on some milestone or accomplishment.

The terms Series A, Series B, and so on refer to the actual shares of the company that are being purchased. Each series of shares can be organized somewhat differently with different terms that all the investors in that round share. A later investor can set up terms that are not favorable to an earlier investor, making it difficult for those earlier investors. For example, a Series D or E investor can really change the structure of the company (disproportionate board seats, for example), and if the capital raise is approved despite objections by a seed round or Series A investor, there is nothing that can be done.

Some investors are really particular about how much money a company should be raising at each funding round.

startup

A company during the first stage of its life is defined as a startup. A company is considered a startup during the time in which the product, corporate structure, customer profile, and growth strategy are determined. This lasts anywhere from zero to fifteen years and is financed, at least in part, by investment, not by customer revenue. At the point a company is able to grow without outside investment, they've left the startup stage and entered the second stage, becoming a growth company. This transition is often fueled by a capital infusion event such as an IPO.

stock

A type of investment security that represents the ownership of a corporation.

stock purchase agreement

The definitive agreement between a company and its shareholders for regulating the sale and transfer of a firm's shares. It covers items such as who has the right of first refusal and provides a mechanism for the purchase (redemption) of the shares of the shareholder who becomes bankrupt, is discharged, resigns, retires, becomes incapacitated, or dies.

stock warrant

A stock warrant is similar to a stock option, because it gives you the right to purchase a company's stock at a specific price and on a specific date. However, a stock warrant differs from an option in two key ways: a stock warrant is issued by the company itself and it exists to help the company raise money.

New shares are issued by the company for the transaction. Unlike a stock option, a stock warrant is issued directly by the company. When a stock option is exercised, the shares usually are received or given by one investor to another. When a stock warrant is exercised, the shares that fulfill the obligation are not received from another investor but directly from the company.

Companies issue stock warrants to raise money. When stock options are bought and sold, the company that owns the stocks does not receive any money from the transactions. However, a stock warrant is a way for a company to raise money through equity (stocks). A stock warrant is a smart way to own shares of a company because a warrant is usually offered at a price lower than that of a stock option. The longest term for an option is two to three years, while a stock warrant can last for up to fifteen years. So, in many cases, a stock warrant can prove to be a better investment than a stock option if mid- to long-term investments are what you seek.

syndicate

Generally speaking, this is a group of people who work together toward a common outcome. For the purposes of startup investing, a syndicate is a collection of investors who work together to fund a company. If multiple investors invest but don't work together to do so, then they're not called a syndicate.

term sheet

An offer of terms to invest in a company. It isn't binding, so it is a useful point of discussion. Sometimes entrepreneurs have a term sheet that they shop around to get investors to sign onto and other times the investors offer a term sheet and compete with each other for the best term sheet. The earlier a company is in the funding process, the more likely they'll be raising funds from a few parties who don't know each other and that often leads to different term sheets being used or to the entrepreneur shopping their term sheet around to multiple investors.

unicorn

Term coined by Aileen Lee to describe startup companies that have a valuation of $1 billion or more.

unicorn employee

An employee at a startup company with a valuation of $1 billion or more.

venture capital firm

Also known as a VC firm, a venture capital firm is an organization comprised of a group of investors, called limited partners (LPs), who pool money together to invest in private companies. The LPs are represented by the general partner (GP) who makes the investment decisions, represents the interests of the LPs, and manages the fund. Venture capital investing is a subset, a small subset, of the private equity industry that focuses on investing in private startup ventures.

venture debt

A loan to a startup company that is operating in part due to the fact that venture capitalists have invested capital. Venture debt funding provides emerging, venture-backed companies with the additional capital needed for equipment and infrastructure build out as well as expansion into new business markets. Venture debt traditionally follows closely after a round of venture capital funding, which lengthens the intervals that an emerging company needs to raise additional venture capital investments.

Venture debt is an attractive option for emerging companies, venture capitalists, and investors. For emerging venture-backed companies, venture debt reduces equity dilution by adding capital to the business without selling stock in exchange for the capital. For venture capitalists, venture debt leverages equity capital investments, which provides stability for a VC's portfolio by adding additional financial sources. In addition, venture debt augments equity returns through its lower capital costs. For the investor, venture debt provides a hybrid alternative to a traditional venture capital fund, combining the predictability of fixed income with the potential returns of venture capital

vetting

A screening process that an investor (usually angel group or VC firm) goes through to determine whether or not a startup has what it takes to become successful and profitable. There is no formula for determining whether a startup company will ultimately be successful or not; however, proper vetting and due diligence are crucial when making informed investment decisions. Vetting is measured by hours of due diligence performed on a startup company.